Written and Illustrated by
TOM PEACOCK

Copyright © 2021 Tom Peacock
All rights reserved
First Edition

PAGE PUBLISHING, INC.
Conneaut Lake, PA

First originally published by Page Publishing 2021

ISBN 978-1-6624-6159-0 (pbk)
ISBN 978-1-6624-6521-5 (hc)
ISBN 978-1-6624-6160-6 (digital)

Printed in the United States of America

To my Grandchildren and all
curious children
everywhere

Bugly,

the ladybug that is more
than just an ordinary bug

Have you ever looked closely at a bug?

**Has a bug ever taken
a close look at you?**

Did you ever wonder what it's like in a bug's world?

Nearly everything is bigger than a bug.

The grass is bigger.

The flowers are bigger.

And other bugs are bigger too!

Some bugs are cute.

And some are scary.

Some bugs are smooth.

And some are hairy.

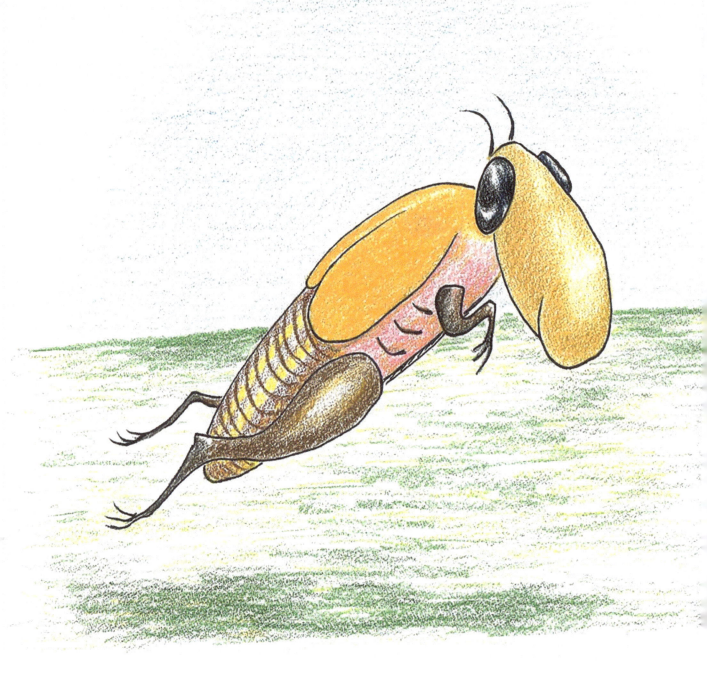

Some bugs hop.

And some bugs crawl.

Some bugs fly.

And some do it all!

Some bugs are helpful.

And some are pests.

Some bugs live in houses.

And some in nests.

Some bugs are black.

And some bugs are green.

Their colors help keep them from being seen.

Some bugs are beautiful.

Some bugs are ugly.

But mostly...

Bugs are just...

BUGLY!

The End

About the Author

Artist/illustrator Tom Peacock grew up on the family ranch in the high desert mountains in eastern Nevada. Working hard and playing hard, he was tagged with the nickname Thunder, which is the signature you see with his cartoon illustrations and earlier artwork.

Pioneer history, the Indian culture, Western wildlife, mustangs, and ranch stock are strong influences in his art. Tom instills the awe he feels when he sees a majestic elk or the reverence felt at the sight of a long-abandoned cabin dwarfed by nature. Humor has always been a part of Tom's art. He has been drawing since childhood, illustrating stories and events with cartoons for high school and college newspapers. While working ranches in Nevada, he completed two Art Instruction School correspondence courses. He finally moved to Colorado to achieve his B.A. in Illustration from Rocky Mountain College of Art and Design in Denver. Since then he has illustrated books, done caricatures, and exhibited his artwork in many fine art shows in Colorado, South Dakota, Nebraska, and Wyoming. His award-winning fine art has hung in galleries and is collected by people locally and internationally.

A kid's curiosity, love of family and friends, the outdoors, and most of all art are what makes sharing a gift the driving force behind Tom's passion.

CPSIA information can be obtained
at www.ICGtesting.com
Printed in the USA
LVHW070752290322
714657LV00002B/17